Studying Elite Political Culture: Problems in Design and Interpretation

Bert A. Rockman

Augsburg College
George Sverdrup Library
Minneapolis, Minnesota 55454

University Center for International Studies
University of Pittsburgh

Acknowledgment

The project which has served to stimulate my thoughts on these matters is the multi-national study of "The Political Cultures of Bureaucrats and Politicians." Those associated with this project are: Joel D. Aberbach, Thomas J. Anton, Samuel J. Eldersveld, Ronald F. Inglehart, and Robert D. Putnam.

I am particularly indebted also to those who read and commented on an earlier draft of this essay. They include: Paul Allen Beck, Robert L. Butterworth, Raymond R. Corrado, Richard W. Cottam, Charles O. Jones, and Robert S. Walters.

Library of Congress Cataloging in Publication Data
Rockman, Bert A
   Studying elite political culture.

   Includes bibliographical references.
   1. Elite (Social sciences) 2. Political sociology.
I. Title.
JC330.R6   301.5'92   76-15708
ISBN 0-916002-11-X

©Copyright 1976, University Center for International Studies
   University of Pittsburgh
All Rights Reserved
Printed in the United States of America
ISBN 0-916002-11-X

Studying Elite Political Culture: Introductory Comments

Though frequently used with insight, the concept of political culture is imbued with ambiguity.[1] This essay explores a set of interrelated theoretical and methodological issues surrounding inquiry into elite political cultures particularly when the techniques of inquiry focus upon individual-level attitudes.

Political culture is posited here as a distal or setting constraint upon a range of available elite behaviors. The following five issues pertaining to the study of elite political culture are discussed:

1. the problem of drawing macro-level inferences from micro-level data;
2. the problem of accounting for discrete policy-related behaviors from attitude data;
3. the problem of reliably interpreting attitudes and values in the absence of proper contextual assessment;
4. the problem of choosing among research design alternatives in examining elite culture and cultural change; and
5. the question of the utility of studies of elite political culture in exploring questions of social and political development.

Permeating all of these issues is a concern with design, interpretation, and levels-of-analysis problems in the study of elite political culture. Because research choices tend to be cumulative in their impact, these problems are interrelated.

My observations stem from my involvement in a cross-national study of the political and social attitudes and beliefs of national bureaucrats and elected politicians. I believe that these observations are generalizable to the study of elite attitudes and to the analysis of elite political culture. In particular, my field experience in interviewing American Federal Executives as part of the larger study serves as an empirical referent point for drawing attention to some broader conceptual, analytic, and methodological problems in the study of elite political culture.

In our study we employed an open-ended survey instrument in an attempt to assess elite beliefs and values with respect to:

1. the role and nature of social and political conflict and the management of conflict;
2. issues relating to political representation, interest articulation, and citizen involvement;
3. the role of administrative and political activity and the atmosphere in which relationships between administrators and politicians are imbedded;
4. the development and evolution of social and political institutions and particularly changes in the character of the party system;
5. the proper role of government in social and economic affairs and the question of decentralization of governmental authority; and
6. the future development of society and aspirations pertaining thereto.

Moreover, we were also interested in how administrators and politicians perceived their own roles and the cognitive styles that they employed in relating to a variety of problems.

By focusing investigation at the level of individual beliefs and values, we sought to uncover patterns of elite norms which broadly surround the policy-making process and a spectrum of intra-elite and elite/citizen relationships. Similarly, a focus on elite values and beliefs could assist our thinking about broader patterns of social change and especially the character of potential elite receptivity or resistance to possible forms of change.² Though specific policy outcomes are neither primarily explanable nor predictable from general attitudinal orientations (i.e., elite political culture), the nature of administrative and political activity over the long haul indeed does derive substantially from the culture and beliefs surrounding these activities. If policy cannot be predicted in specific terms, the elite culture that surrounds policy-making helps to demarcate the boundaries of possible and probable policy outcomes.

Elite Political Culture: Drawing Macro Inferences from Micro Data

The concept "political culture" is hazy and terribly imprecise and, strictly speaking, it may not even enjoy the status of a real concept. However, in terms of its connotive value, "political culture" implies the existence of deeply ingrained but distal values and supporting belief structures that permeate political and governmental activities in not always clearly specifiable ways. Political culture holds interpretive value, then, rather than a direct explanatory one for understanding how government and politics function within certain contexts.³

Further, political culture is a systems-level concept not an individual-level one though it is derived in large part from individual beliefs and values. In other words, while the actual units of analysis are individual-level, the level of analytic inference is ultimately systemic. The "cultural elements," in short, represent conceptual inferences from the observables. Political culture, in this sense, is a conceptual vehicle for dealing with macro-level concerns via micro-level data.

The disparity that often exists in the macro-social sciences between the actual *units of analysis* (i.e., the empirical units of observation) and *levels of analytic inference* is especially encountered in studies utilizing survey or individual-interview techniques. While measurement is undertaken at the individual level, meaningful system or relational inferences must go beyond the mere aggregation of these individual properties. Surely, this dilemma affects all studies that attempt to probe cultural patterns by means of individual-level measurement techniques. The linkage problems across levels can hardly be ignored. Attitudes and values are attributes of individuals, but their importance for political research usually pertains to collective social phenomena.⁴ The political researcher, then, is often in the position of justifying the importance of examining subjective aspects of politics (i.e., beliefs and values) in terms of macro-level phenomena, though he frequently does not have direct empirical indicators for these phenomena. Consequently, the connection between attitudes and systemic events is often meandering and tenuous.⁵

Even at the level of the individual, the more specifically targeted an attitude is to a discrete measurable behavior, the more likely it is that the attitude and the behavior will be directly correlated.⁶ To the extent that some form of discrete and specifiable behavior (e.g., a vote) can be measured at the same level as an attitude (i.e., the individual level), the more likely it is that particular intervening variables can be specified and analytically controlled. Conversely, the less specificity between attitude and behavior, the more likely it is that other variables will mediate the attitude-behavior nexus, introducing "contingent" or "interactive" effects.⁷ As Greenstein has noted, no direct relationship can be assumed between personality structures, political belief systems, individual political action, and aggregate political structures and processes.⁸

In sum, an imprecise sense as to what attitudinal data may yield with respect to complex political-system properties and behavior representing another level of inference results especially from (1) the frequent absence of an explicitly measured dependent variable to which attitudes can be referenced and (2) the frequent inability to clearly specify which structural and contextual variables mediate attitudes and how they do so in the absence of time-series data.

The problem of linking general patterns of elite attitudes and symbolic values to system-level consequences is no small one indeed. Collective behaviors or events presumed to be dependent upon a particular array of attitudes are often measured irrespective of their theoretically specified sequence,[9] if they are measured at all. Clearly, one of the key problems involved is to provide an empirical structure that corresponds to a theoretical one. Thus, to the extent that theoretical inferences are system-oriented while the actual units of observation are individual-level, the latter permits only speculative inferences to be made about system-level properties.

Attitudes and Policy

Our investigation into the political and social attitudes of American Federal Executives was directed more to symbolic elements than to opinions concerning highly specified policy options. Our primary concern was with standards, principles, and perceptions that potentially may govern behavior. The search for general attitudinal patterns over a broad range of concerns, however, is not especially compatible with a high degree of behavioral specification. Specific policy positions advanced or favored by administrators are not necessarily linearly deducible from the articulation of general value premises. Behavior, after all, depends upon opportunities. Policy-related choices are more or less structured by particular constraints. Rarely are the decisional stimuli confronting an administrator (or politician) easily and immediately definable in philosophic or symbolic terms. The behavior of administrators especially is hemmed in by a variety of situational and structural constraints. As one administrative official claimed, "I used to spend more time deciding whether I'd get the six dollar wash-and-wear shirt or the seven dollar wash-and-wear shirt, than I do on a 20 billion dollar decision." Thus, as Warner and his associates have pointed out:

> The civilian executive is a member of a multiple, massive, and highly structured formal organization. Always contextually of great significance to all his actions are distinctions of this order: bureau level-department level; chief-deputy; headquarters-field; executive-legislative. Both cognitive and unreflective action must be geared to these referents of explicitly described and formally codified relationships. It is the exactness of these relationships rather than their complexity, that is most typical of the federal world — and for that matter, all worlds of large organizations.[10]

While the exactness of these relationships can be overstated, it is still the case that considerable amounts of administrative activity are highly structured and regulated. These structural constraints obviously mediate attitude-behavior relationships.

The achievement of a high degree of predictive accuracy from attitudes to behavior requires a different set of research choices grounded in a different set of research objectives than those which we pursued. For instance, highly specified policy areas and issues would have to be dealt with. By contrast with our open-ended and semi-focused questions, a strategy aimed at enhancing behavioral predictability would require the interviewer in his questions to replicate the situational contingencies and structural constraints confronting the subject. In order to replicate these contingencies to achieve a greater isomorphism between attitudinal response and behavioral option, the researcher would have to possess considerable amounts of highly specific policy-related information *prior* to the time of the interview. A series of forced-choice items might then be especially appropriate. But obtaining specific policy information of this sort for each respondent would necessitate a whole series of specific case studies or would require concentrating all of the respondents within a particular policy or program area. Maximizing the attitude-behavior link in a predictive sense for each individual requires the researcher to be well steeped in a particular program area and to know in advance what the relevant array of choice options might be for any administrator. Such procedures are especially appropriate for testing decision-making models.[11] Unless a formal decision-making model is specified and evaluated empirically, however, the prediction of discrete behaviors among elites is generally of greater concern to journalists than to social scientists whose informational resources are typically insufficiently rich for these purposes.

Concern with predictive accuracy alone, however, inevitably leads to the detailed examination of trees. The more *direct* the linkage to behavior one wishes to draw, the more it becomes necessary to elaborate and specify a large number of situational and structural predictors. The more specific the predictors, the greater the confidence in predicting behavior. But the function of a theory is to provide some measure of conceptual economy. A high degree of behavioral predictability from attitudes at the individual level may well be purchased at the price of theoretical concepts and analytic coherence. Moreover, concern only at the micro level leads to an obsession with predicting individual reactions to specific events. In psychological terms this can be edifying, but political analysis is also more than the study of individual choice-making. A primary interest in inferences pertaining to the political system or to institutional sectors therein requires a strategy capable of eliciting broader, if more distal, attitudinal orientations than one that seeks to maximize predictability over short-run behaviors. Consequently, a concern with the distribution of general attitude patterns is more useful in dealing with inferences across levels of analysis.

Our motivating interest, therefore, in employing the concept of elite political culture was to capture the patterning of a broad array of elite orientations rather than to predict specific, discrete behavior. In this sense, an elite political culture comprises a broad and interwoven texture of subjective orientations that help us to understand the broad values and expectations that enter into the policy process, even if these cannot be captured in operational detail. Thus, elite political culture assists us in interpreting how governmental and political institutions operate by emphasizing the values that color their operation. By enabling us to discern the normative and perceptual baggage of elites, focusing on political culture also helps us to assess how elites may respond to various kinds of change. So, despite the fact that "A determination of what behavior actually occurs depends on a detailed study of intervening variables ...",[12] the concept of elite political culture may offer a more coherent tool by which to interpret behavioral patterns. Finally, it should be noted that "elite culture" is best addressed to comparative cross-system analyses because the attitude orientations implied by the concept are sufficiently general that they are likely to assume greater variance as the stratifying variables themselves become more general, e.g., country as opposed to administrative sub-unit.

Attitude Patterns and Contextual Assessment

When political culture is studied through individual-level attitude research, the problem of relating attitudes to contexts arises. This is a two-pronged problem, both aspects of which raise the issue of the valid interpretation and translation of elite attitude patterns.[13] Briefly, the first issue concerns the question of the *derivation* of individual level attitudes; the second issue concerns the question of what system-level *inferences* can be drawn from such attitudes. *These issues are related in the sense that the inferences to be drawn may well be dependent upon our understanding as to the derivations of the observed attitudes.*

Context and the Explanation of Attitudes

To hold certain attitudes and values, in a sense, is also to summarize a particular kind of learning experience.[14] Because those learning experiences are enormously complex, we are probably all subject from time to time to slipping into conceptual reification when dealing with "attitudes" and "values" and, thus, granting them an autonomy and sturdiness which may be ill-placed. This may be especially the case when we are limited to cross-sectional observation.

The problem, then, is how we may account for given attitude patterns. *The concept "political culture" almost presupposes a certain level of durability in these patterns – some constancy in pattern that may or may not be there at the level of the individual.* For example, is an official's attitudes toward something like citizen participation in governmental programs formed in personal cost-benefit terms, as an element of a larger social ideology, as the result of some proximate experience, or as part of a broader collective historical experience in which values about popular participation have been formed?[15] The question seems almost metaphysical since the examination of aggregated attitude patterns does not lend itself to ferreting out individual sources of attitude development in this manner. Yet the question remains. I recollect vividly one administrator whom I had interviewed waxing eloquently, if abstractly, about the importance of active, sustained citizen participation if technocratic rule by bureaucrats was to be avoided. It was only a short time after this interview that I discovered that the program headed by this official was being evaluated adversely by both the individual's agency and by the Office of Management and Budget. His potential levers apparently lay with the rather well-organized outside clientele affected by the program that he headed. For any administrator, then, his performance of a given role, his location within a specific organizational unit or task context, and his experiences within that context may well be decisive in determining how he will respond to and interpret what the theorist may regard as a more general stimulus.[16]

The problem, of course, leads one into the analysis of individual value systems, but that falls more readily into the domain of psychological investigation.[17] Individual level theories of cognition and attitude development requiring fairly intensive longitudinal analyses of individuals with respect to the sources of their learning can provide useful links to political analysis. Without longitudinal analyses and massive analytic disaggregation, though, *inferences pertaining to the actual assimilating processes that are going on at the level of the individual are hard to come by.* A heavy emphasis on causal inference with respect to individual attitude development tends to move the analytic focus away from the aggregating concept of "elite culture." There is, perhaps, an inescapable disjuncture between attempts to specify individual-level models of socialization and attempts to *account for* attitude patterns among *classes of actors* by the broad influences of collective historical events or even the somewhat narrower constraints of role settings. The former tends to lead us back to the micro level; the latter to institutional and macro-level social and political influences.

The elite culture approach, in sum, tends to employ rather broad stratifying variables to account for political and social experiences. Viewed in this perspective, the relevance of cross-national analysis is clear. For cross-nationally, one would expect to discover variations in elite outlook as a function of: (1) differences in broader social and cultural values; (2) differences in patterns of institutional relationship; and (3) differences in the level and character of socio-political development. *Within a one-country sample,* attitudes acquired in the context of organizational roles are especially likely to account for variation in outlook. Therefore, the potential importance of role variables cannot be ignored. Nonetheless, organizational role must be viewed against the backdrop of the broader society. In other words, an emphasis on elite culture may tend to *summarize* the kinds of experiences and relational patterns that administrative officials in a particular society typically encounter. In this sense, the "whole" of these experiences may be more meaningful *over the long run* than the examination of particular variations owing to organizational context.

Context and Inferences from Attitudes

Looking at elite political culture as an aggregative concept leads us from the problem of contextually specifying the sources of individual level attitudes to the problem of contextually assessing their aggregate meaning.[18] Lehman notes here that:

> ... the most fruitful use of culture is not as an isolated independent variable ... Rather, political culture and culture in general are most productively treated as specifying variables for understanding political behavior and structural changes. A specifying variable has only a 'modified' explanatory impact; i.e., it 'specifies' the conditions under which more strategic correlations will exist in greater or lesser intensity. Seen in this light, culture should be viewed as one of the conditions of the broader 'context' which encourage or inhibit the interaction of social system properties.[19]

Lehman's argument is compelling because it points to the problem of drawing interpretive inferences from isolated attitudes. Determining which behavioral propensities are likely to arise from given orientations obviously depends upon how particular attitude and value patterns interrelate and upon an understanding of the context in which such patterns exist. Any particular value pattern isolated from context can be interpreted in multiple ways. For example, a high incidence of trust between administrators and politicians may result in different behavioral patterns, depending upon the role of other variables. Administrators who place very high degrees of trust in elected politicians and external interest groups may well wind up supplanting administrative criteria in policy implementation with particularistic political criteria.[20] On the other hand, if, as Torodd Strand points out, there exists in Sweden mutual trust between administrators and politicians arising out of a value consensus oriented around problem solving,[21] long-range planning may well be enhanced. Apparent similarities in attitude patterns across political contexts, then, may have distinctly different consequences. Lehman's suggestion is that the discovery of such patterns should lead us to look to other systemic properties in order to understand the derivation of these patterns and to consider their consequences. Aggregate value patterns, in short, reflect in some measure the ways in which social and political institutions historically have worked.

Elite political culture, therefore, is but one point of entry to understanding the operation of complex political systems. Its utility as a point of entry is that it should direct us toward the need to develop a richer understanding of the historical forces and institutional evolutions that have shaped and are shaping societal development.

Elite Political Culture: Research Alternatives

If an elite culture analytically constitutes something more than the aggregation of individual properties, then why direct inquiry to the level of the individual? There are undoubtedly alternative procedures. *Analytic case studies* of policy processes are perhaps a most obvious alternative procedure by which to examine an elite political culture. Policy case studies can be analyzed over time in order to extract normative and perceptual inferences from repetitive behaviors. They can also be analyzed across systems to establish comparative bases for drawing inferences. The analytic case approach possesses a number of virtues that especially enhance our understanding about relational patterns in policy making and implementation. This approach essentially starts with behavioral data and works back to inferences about the subjective elements. Taken as an "exclusive" point of entry into the study of elite culture, however, case studies of policy processes also have certain limitations.

One major problem posed by the case approach is that it limits generalization. The case study technique requires a detailed knowledge on the part of the investigator of the issues being examined and an intensive access to a potentially wide array of actors. The trade-offs for the investigator are very real here because a high degree of detailed knowledge can be obtained typically only within a very limited universe of policy domains. Thus, the case approach creates a rich and elaborate explanatory apparatus for dealing with a range of interactions within a given policy domain, but the richness may come at the cost of broader analytic coherence. Always, the question — what the case is a case of — has to be addressed. The rich immersion into policy process that the case approach affords tends to narrow either the range of policy domains capable of being investigated or the range of relevant influences. The former constraint creates some difficulties in generalizing across policy domains and presents some difficulties for cross-national investigation. The latter constraint means that the case approach generally does not deal directly with broader *distal* influences that may permeate in subtle ways the interactions being examined.[22]

The most important implication of this second point is that the case approach *may fail to provide analytic levers by which to assess possible trends* affecting the policy process and, more generally, the atmosphere in which governments operate. Directly focusing on subjective elements (i.e., beliefs and values of elites) provides a more direct opportunity to consider changes in elite values and perceptions. Thus, while the inductive orientation of case studies may impair our ability to discern general characteristics of interaction from those patterns which are specific to each case,[23] focusing upon the subjective elements of elite culture more readily lends itself to the discovery of general patterns initially and helps to provide a context in which policy behaviors can be examined. The gain, particularly for comparative analysis, seems justifiable in terms of analytic economy.

Further, if motivational ambiguity arises when inferences have to be made between symbolic attitudes and behavioral patterns, i.e., the problem of "the intervening variables," it also arises, though in different form, when we attempt to infer motivation and preference from behavioral data only. To the extent, therefore, that elite culture suggests important setting values and beliefs for understanding the character of policy interactions, complex inferences with respect to behavior in identifiable contexts may be built with greater facility upon the subjective base than can the subjective elements be reconstructed from behavioral patterns.[24] Moreover, important changes in the cultural setting may be taking place which a focus upon behavioral patterns alone is not likely to reveal.

From the standpoint of examining elite political culture, the individual-level subjective approach and the policy study approach ideally should complement one another. They should not, therefore, be viewed as mutually exclusive; rather, they provide different kinds of information. The "black box" of decision-making processes represents the short run arena for assessing the role of broader setting influences such as elite culture. The elite culture approach would suggest to us, for example, that if bureaucrats emphasize pluralist values and political access from the outside and if they view political conflict as valuable, then they are likely to facilitate an active involvement of external interest groups in the administrative process and to view themselves as an integral part of the political process. How such broad orientations actually facilitate or constrain behavior in the "black box" of policy making and implementation is a subject of inquiry best suited for case analysis.

In short, while the case study approach can yield rich insight into elite perceptions and norms permeating policy-related activity, it may lack the requisite analytic breadth and generality of the attitudinal approach. The two approaches should link to one another, though. Analytic case studies of policy especially can provide a means of assessing some possible operational consequences of elite culture.

Any approach to the investigation of elite political culture, however, will be limited in part by static qualities of observation and measurement. Cross-sectional data obviously provide less generalizing power and, hence, less analytic utility than do time-series data. In mass survey research, dynamic panel techniques can be employed fruitfully over fairly short intervals of time. But in dealing with as expansive a concept as elite political culture it makes theoretical sense to scatter the data points over substantially greater distances of time. Changes in patterns of elite culture require extended time frames. In order to siphon off circumstantial influences from more fundamental characteristics of elite culture, time-series data are clearly advantageous.

When samples have to be taken over large time intervals it is generally not feasible to employ techniques such as panel analysis that are aimed at studying individual change. But it is also not necessary to be consumed by the problem of individual change in studying changes in aspects of elite political culture. To repeat an earlier point that is also relevant here, the concept of elite political culture is essentially aggregative. Techniques aimed at the dynamics of individual change are not essential for examining net change. Thus, multiple cross-section samples scattered over large time intervals from similar universes hold most practical promise for analyzing change and stability in patterns of elite culture.

A broader issue, though, remains to be addressed. To what extent do governmental elites make a difference? Therefore, are elite values and beliefs worth studying? The issue, if fundamental, is not always clear. The next section of this essay attempts to place the role of elite political culture in a broad perspective of social development and change. To do so with great precision remains an elusive goal, nonetheless.

Elite Political Culture: Explanatory Pay-Offs

The thrust of many of my preceding comments has been directed to the notion that the concept of "elite culture" is most useful as an interpretive rather than behaviorally specific predictive tool. To isolate an elite political culture primarily as a predictive mechanism is not only simplistic in an analytic sense, but it also gives to the manipulable aspects of politics (i.e., leadership) an autonomy and independent strength that is fundamentally misleading. Politics, after all, is a fairly marginal activity in terms of social development, especially in constitutionalist systems where demands for responsiveness dilute the autonomy of public officials.[25] To say this is not to diminish the importance of the margins, however. Rather, it requires taking note of the largely nonmanipulable features of any society — its historical and physical situation and the nature of its social and political institutions. From the standpoint of elite behavior, the constraints imposed by these features are significant. So also are those that spring from mass cultural phenomena. The importance of these constraints clearly should not be underestimated. Figure 1 represents a rough attempt to sketch these broad systemic relationships. These relationships suggest the multiplicity of constraints shaping and limiting the impact of elite beliefs and values.

With respect to the kinds of limitations that they impose, they are first likely to define an acceptable range of possible solutions to problems. For example, the impact of physical resources is often evident. A mobilizing elite culture probably will make little impact in terms of modernization if there are too few resources with which to modernize. Broader cultural considerations are also imposing. An elite culture that emphasizes government planning and controls and widening spheres of public activity at the expense of private activity is unlikely to be legitimized if the broader society is nurtured in abundance, competitiveness, individualism, and private consumption. A broad privatizing cultural pattern may then conflict with governmental capacities to plan and marshal resources for social policy.

The particular nature of these systemic relationships will confront different societies with different sets of problems. The character of these problems can impose greater or lesser constraints on leadership and they are also likely to color elite beliefs and values. If intensely polarized conflict exists in a society, for instance, it is likely to lead to policy stalemate and the potential of civil disorder. The supply of political resources may diminish rapidly under such conditions.[26] One result may be institutional devitalization and a growing incapacity to aggregate demands effectively into channels of responsible political choice. Achieving social peace under these conditions will require diverting energies away from institutional capacities to engage in long-run planning and policy coordination.

The institutional structures of government and of the broader political arena, themselves products of historical circumstance, also can constrain or facilitate government action. Institutions such as federalism, divided authority, and local autonomy fragment power and require a heavy dependence upon persuasion, compromise, and bargaining. In this regard, the American system has a blocking rather than mobilizational bias. The effect is to exact a substantial price in terms of

FIGURE 1
LOCATING ELITE POLITICAL CULTURE WITHIN A SYSTEMS PERSPECTIVE

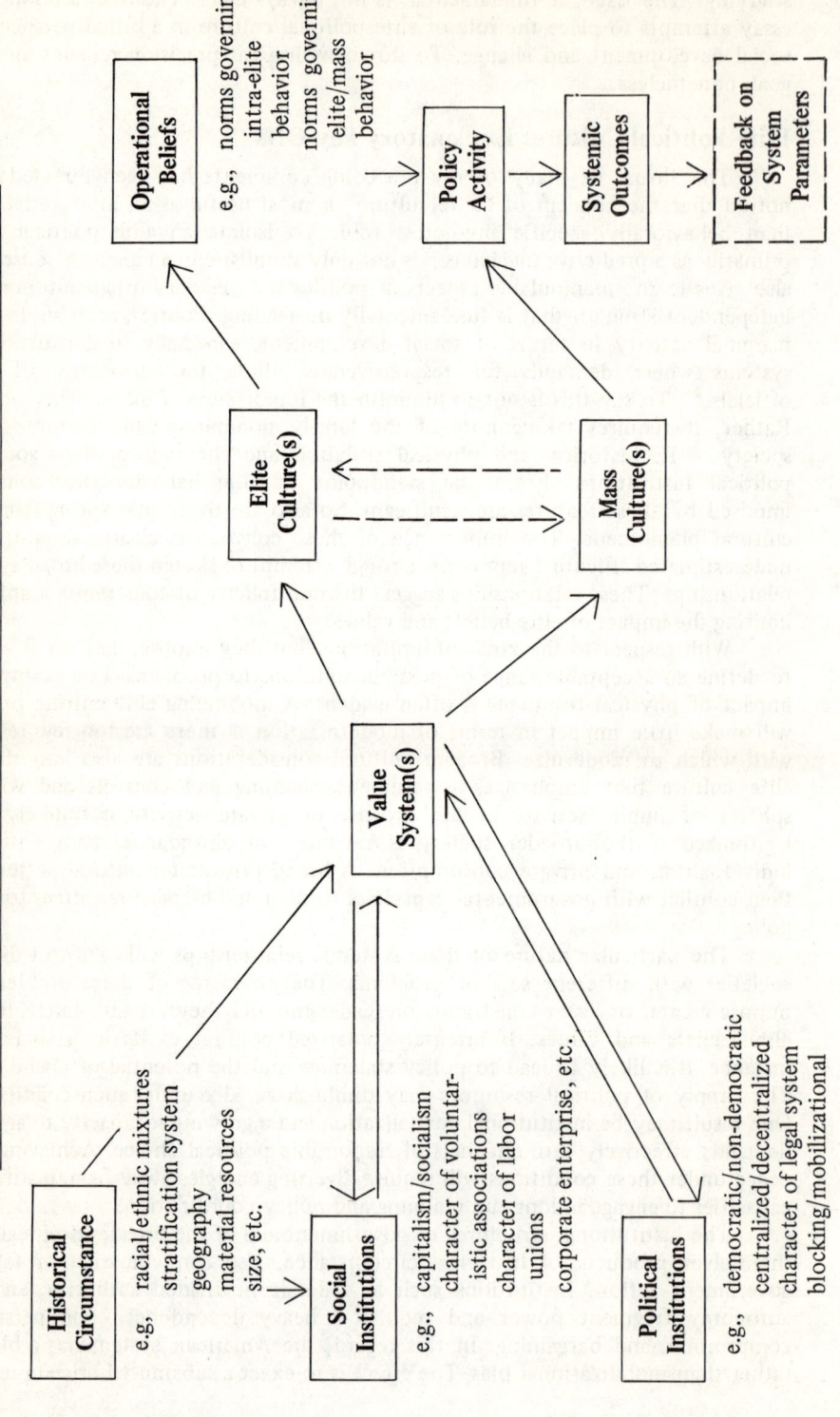

policy planning and coherence. Huntington, for instance, observes that:

> The passion of the Founding Fathers for the division of power, for setting ambition against ambition, for creating a constitution with a complicated system of balances exceeding that of any other is well known. Everything is bought at a price, however, and as many Englishmen have pointed out, one apparent price of the division of power is governmental inefficiency.[27]

In the absence of shared values, a system characterized by attributes such as these tends toward inertia.

Finally, of course, the less "statist" a society the more likely it is that nonpublic elites will exert greater aggregate influence over decisions and policy agendas affecting the commonweal. To that extent, leadership encompasses a broader sphere than public officialdom. In brief, the more pluralized are the sources of leadership in a society, the greater are the constraints potentially attending to the exercise of public leadership.

The variety of systemic parameters discussed above tend to define roughly the perimeters within which public officials can act effectively. Therefore, elite political culture becomes a useful organizing concept only in the context of understood parameters. *The utility of focusing on elite orientations is that they help us to understand how elites perceive and cope with these system parameters.*

We may conclude, then, that: (1) the course of social development does not hinge entirely on political processes alone; (2) political processes or their outcomes are hardly a direct function of the attitudes and values expressed by elites; and (3) the attitudinal dispositions of elite sectors are nonetheless important in order to develop an understanding as to how elites perceive and respond to the "givens" of their environment. What opportunities are seized or not, of course, will depend upon how elites perceive and respond to those "givens." Investigating the values and beliefs of governmental elites represents but one piece of a very complicated puzzle. Nevertheless, elite culture can help us to understand how some of the other pieces fit together. Though a thorough understanding as to *how* elite perceptions and values color governmental response depends upon additional modes of inquiry, we can concur with Philip Jacob that "... the values that leaders hold make a difference in what they do, and hence in their effectiveness as agents of social development, and ... that social development is at least in part a function of political leadership."[28]

Summary

Five general issues affecting research design, interpretation, and analysis problems in the study of elite political culture have been raised. While these concerns stem from my involvement in a cross-national investigation of bureaucrats and politicians, they are also likely to be generalizable to other elite attitude inquiries and to more general issues attending the study of elite political culture.

First, there is the problem of *drawing macro-level inferences from micro-level data.* The concept of political culture implies a system-level concern, but system-level inferences cannot be drawn solely from individual-level units of observation, that is, from attitude data collected through interviews. The difficulties normally attendant to drawing inferences across levels are further exacerbated by the conceptual ambiguity of political culture itself. The concept, being essentially connotive, is likely to be of little *direct* value in explaining short run system-level phenomena. Clearly, the linkage between individual-level attitudes and system-level events requires a host of specifying variables. Only speculative inferences therefore can be made between the individual-level data and theoretical statements of system-level "effects."

A *second issue* deals with the *relationship between individual-level attitudes and invididual behavior with respect to policy choices*. Again, in order to account for specific policy-related behaviors of individual members of the sample, a multitude of detailed specifying variables must be considered. Unfortunately, this comes at the expense of theoretical generality. In studies of elite attitudes there is a necessary distinction to be made between predictive specificity and theoretical generality. The more general the theoretical thrust is, the more distal its impact; hence, theoretical generality tends toward behavioral indeterminacy at the individual level. There is no "best" solution in the abstract. The choice between capturing general orientations or specifying individual behaviors must be made according to the character of one's research objectives. Focusing on elite political culture, however, leads toward an emphasis upon general orientations. Because general attitude orientations tend to assume greater variance the more general are the stratifying variables, the study of elite political culture makes particular sense in cross-national terms.

A *third issue* deals with the problem of indeterminacies in attitude data in another way. In particular, it deals with *the problem of context in interpreting attitudes*. Though the concept of elite culture implies the existence of deeply held collective values, to what extent can we be sure that these have been captured? Without detailing a dynamic process model of socialization, we cannot be sure when dealing at the level of the individual. But the concept of elite culture is aggregative. Thus, it is especially suitable for contrasting perceptual and value *modalities* across political systems. This leads to another issue in contextual interpretation. Namely, to what extent can similar attitude patterns across societal contexts be interpreted in the same way? Do they imply similar consequences and are they developed out of similar learning experiences? The problem is thorny and probably incapable of being fully resolved. To resort to "context" as a basis for interpretation, in effect, means resorting to a set of unspecified variables. In the end, however, an understanding of how contextual variables operate is important because elite culture is best employed as an interpretive tool. Its virtue may be to amplify our understanding of context by directing our attention to historical and institutional development.

A *fourth issue concerns the matter of research tactics in studying elite political culture.* How do we proceed to infer the existence of certain reasonably durable perceptual and value influences on elite behavior? Though we utilized an open-ended survey procedure, another alternative discussed was the analytic case approach to policy making and implementation which focuses on decision-making activity. By examining patterns of behavior, it may be possible to draw inferences about the values and beliefs of relevant actors. For the study of elite political culture the case approach, however, suffers from boundary problems when applied comparatively and may limit generalization under other conditions. Most important, it is often quite difficult to infer attitude patterns from behavioral activity. Analytic economy, therefore, may be gained by building upon a foundation of elite beliefs and values. The case approach, however, can provide an important operational link by which to assess the role of elite culture. It has been argued here that the attitude and case approaches should best be thought of as complementing one another rather than being mutually exclusive.

Still, when probing elite political culture through interview techniques, it is difficult to distinguish in cross-sectional research between outlooks induced by temporal circumstance and those of deeper underlying significance. This problem plagues all cross-sectional attitude research. The analysis of cultural change is undertaken most effectively with time-series data. Since large intervals of time are required to examine cultural change at the elite level, sampling techniques aimed at examining attitude change among individuals are not feasible. Emphasis, therefore, must be placed upon aggregate or marginal change rather than individual change. The problem of the durability of individual attitudes remains disturbing but not crucial to the investigation of elite political culture.

Finally, and perhaps the most important issue of all, is the matter of what elite culture can tell the student of politics. Politics is only one of the forces shaping social development. It is perhaps even a marginal force. Moreover, though the relative impact of "governmental elites" will vary according to the social and political traditions and structures of a society, the manipulative role of leadership in any society is limited to some degree. Despite this, "elite culture" can lead toward an understanding of how societal resources will be dealt with. For example, when confronted with similar problems of economic development, the governing elites of Russia and India chose different paths. Similarly, faced with the more liberating effects of economic affluence (or the more recent jolts of scarcity coexisting with capital wealth), an understanding as to how governmental elites in the post-industrial societies of the West may respond to different types of challenges can be facilitated by the exploration of "elite political culture."

The purpose of this essay has been to point out a number of analytic, conceptual, and methodological dilemmas confronting this exploration.

FOOTNOTES

1. See, for instance, Sidney Verba, "Comparative Political Culture," in Lucian W. Pye and Sidney Verba (eds.), *Political Culture and Political Development* (Princeton, N.J.: Princeton University Press, 1965) 512-560; Lucian W. Pye, "Culture and Political Science: Problems in the Evaluation of the Concept of Political Culture," in Louis Schneider and Charles Bonjean (eds.), *The Idea of Culture in the Social Sciences* (Cambridge, England: Cambridge University Press, 1973) 65-76; and Edward W. Lehman, "On the Concept of Political Culture: A Theoretical Reassessment," *Social Forces,* 50 (March 1972) 361-370. See also Robert D. Putnam, *The Beliefs of Politicians: Ideology, Conflict and Democracy in Britain and Italy* (New Haven: Yale University Press, 1973) especially chapters 1 and 2.
2. See, especially, M. Donald Hancock and Gideon Sjoberg (eds.), *Politics in the Post-Welfare State: Responses to the New Individualism* (New York: Columbia University Press, 1972); and Richard L. Simpson, "Beyond Rational Bureaucracy: Changing Values and Social Integration in Post-Industrial Society," *Social Forces,* 51 (September, 1972) 1-6.
3. This is a point addressed by others. See, in this regard, Verba, *op. cit.,* and Lehman, *op. cit.*
4. For an insightful analysis of the relationship between individual, aggregate, and contextual properties, see Douglas Price, "Micro and Macro-Politics: Notes on Research Strategy," in Oliver Garceau (ed.), *Political Research and Political Theory* (Cambridge: Harvard University Press, 1968) especially pp. 124-140.

   In the context of political culture studies, it is also worthwhile to ponder Edward Lehman's contention that:

   > ... although it may be advantageous to measure properties of culture by sampling individuals it must be borne in mind that cultural items have been conceptualized as essentially *supramembership* in nature so that their analytic status does not flow directly from the properties of individual actors.

   See Lehman, *op. cit.,* 362. Emphases are in the original.
5. For a study which crosses both levels and systems in an attempt to explore the relationship between values and aggregate community activity, see Philip Jacob, *et al., Values and the Active Community: A Cross-National Study of the Influences of Local Leadership* (New York: The Free Press, 1971). The subtitle is somewhat misleading, however, since there is no way to account specifically for leadership influence on community activity (the dependent variable). Recursiveness must be assumed under a theory positing the influence of attitudes on collective behavior. But especially when measurement is at different levels it becomes exceedingly difficult to meet the test of recursiveness. See, especially, Chapters 1 and 2.
6. See, for instance, Martin Fishbein, "Attitudes and the Prediction of Behavior," in Martin Fishbein (ed.), *Readings in Attitude Theory and Measurement* (New York: John Wiley, 1967) 477-492.
7. See, Howard J. Ehrlich, "Attitudes, Behavior, and the Intervening Variables," *American Sociologist,* 4 (February, 1969) 29-34.
8. See, Fred Greenstein, *Personality and Politics* (Chicago: Markham, 1969) 124-127. Students of political socialization, for example, have discovered how difficult it is to predict with real precision implications for system stability from

diffuse patterns of childhood support for political institutions. See *inter alia,* David Easton and Jack Dennis, *Children in the Political System* (New York: McGraw-Hill, 1969); Jack Dennis, *et al.,* "Political Socialization to Democratic Orientations in Four Western Systems," *Comparative Political Studies,* 1 (April 1968) 71-101; and Jack Dennis, *et al.,* "Support for Nation and Government Among English Children," *British Journal of Political Science,* 1 (January 1971) 25-48. For some critiques dealing with the "open-ended" system implications of childhood socialization to political authority, see Reid R. Reading, "Is Easton's Systems-Persistence Framework Useful? A Research Note," *Journal of Politics,* 34 (February 1972) 258-267; and Dennis Kavanagh, "Allegiance among English Children: A Dissent," *British Journal of Political Science,* 2 (January 1972) 127-131. For a more general critique of the linkage problems, see Donald D. Searing, Joel J. Schwartz, and Alden E. Lind, "The Structuring Principle: Political Socialization and Belief Systems," *American Political Science Review,* 67 (June 1973) 415-432.

9. For an incisive discussion of this problem, see Robert Burrowes, "Theory Si! Data No! A Decade of Cross-National Political Research," *World Politics,* 25 (October 1972) especially 133-141.

10. W. Lloyd Warner, *et al., The American Federal Executive* (New Haven: Yale University Press, 1963) 238.

11. In some respects such a procedure using computer simulation techniques rather than interviews is utilized by Cyert and March in order to test specific components of a general decision-making model. See Richard M. Cyert and James G. March, *A Behavioral Theory of the Firm* (Englewood Cliffs, N. J.: Prentice-Hall, 1963). Also see John P. Crecine, *Governmental Problem-Solving: A Computer Simulation of Municipal Budgeting* (Chicago: Rand McNally, 1969). A useful description of what one needs to know beforehand in order to specify alternative models is provided in Donald R. Matthews, "From the Senate to Simulation," in Oliver Walter (ed.), *Political Scientists at Work* (Belmont, California: Duxbury Press, 1971) 9-27.

12. See James C. Scott, *Political Ideology in Malaysia: Reality and the Beliefs of an Elite* (New Haven: Yale University Press, 1968) 30.

13. The problem of validation exists, as Anderson observes, ". . . whenever research asks the 'same' question of people with differing backgrounds." See R. Bruce W. Anderson, "On the Comparability of Meaningful Stimuli in Cross-National Research," *Sociometry,* 30 (June 1967) 124.

14. McClosky and Schaar, for example, account for anomic responses in terms of a failure of socialization. In their formulation, those who exhibit anomic attitudinal characteristics have failed to encounter successfully the norms of mainstream socialization. In a somewhat similar vein, Gamson and Modigliani conclude that higher levels of information about foreign affairs generally reflect a learning of "mainstream" positions. See Herbert McClosky and John H. Schaar, "Psychological Dimensions of Anomy," *American Sociological Review,* 30 (February 1965) 14-40; and William A. Gamson and Andre Modigliani, "Knowledge and Foreign Policy Opinions: Some Models for Consideration," *Public Opinion Quarterly,* 30 (Summer 1966) 187-199.

15. To be sure, these considerations interact. The relationship between modal social and collective values, role-related opportunities and experiences, and the absorption of particular situational experiences within an individual's belief system are incredibly difficult to disentangle.

16. See, especially, the organizational model in Cyert and March, *op. cit.* The model is predicated on organizational and sub-unit learning. One important assumption of the model is that sub-unit experiences will affect goal definition. For some interesting evidence as to how organizational locus affects the individual's definition of goals, see DeWitt C. Dearborn and Herbert A. Simon, "A Note on the Department Identification of Executives," *Sociometry,* 21 (June 1958) 140-144. For an interesting study suggesting the importance of task-unit as a predictor of the strength, but not the direction, of certain foreign policy orientations, see Andrew K. Semmel, *Some Correlates of Foreign Policy Attitudes Among U.S. Foreign Service Officers* (Unpublished Ph.D. thesis, The University of Michigan, 1972).

17. See, for instance, Milton Rokeach, *Beliefs, Attitudes, and Values* (San Francisco: Jossey-Bass, 1969). Rokeach's analytic concern is with the *organization of personal belief systems.*

18. This is an ancient dilemma of cross-national research. For some penetrating and sobering comments on the problem of contextual assessment of cross-national data, see *inter alia,* Joseph LaPalombara, "Parsimony and Empiricism in Comparative Politics: An Anti-Scholastic View," in Robert T. Holt and John E. Turner (eds.), *The Methodology of Comparative Research* (New York: The Free Press, 1970) 123-149; Frederick W. Frey, "Cross-Cultural Survey Research in Political Science," in Holt and Turner, *op. cit.,* especially 187-294; Sidney Verba, "Some Dilemmas in Comparative Research," *World Politics,* 20 (October 1967) 111-127; Fred I. Greenstein and Sidney G. Tarrow, "The Study of French Political Socialization: Toward the Revocation of Paradox," *World Politics,* 22 (October 1969) 95-137. Greenstein and Tarrow comment that:

> Fixed choice and other relatively structured and unprobing ways of eliciting response are more problematic in cross-cultural research than in research within a single culture. The wider the cultural range of the populations being studied, the more difficult it is to know whether respondents who check the 'same' questionnaire alternative in fact mean the same thing.

See Greenstein and Tarrow, *op. cit.,* 131. Anderson's cautionary words — especially in studies without behavioral dependent variables — are well taken here:

> A common means of validating personality instruments is by comparison of responses made by subjects who exhibit behavioral differences. Similar findings in cross-cultural comparison are often assumed to indicate cultural differences without a comparable concern for behavioral validation. If, on the other hand, *equivalent* responses are obtained from a multi-societal investigation they are often uncritically attributed to cultural universals. It will be noted that in either of these situations stimulus equivalence is assumed, and conclusions are based on the obtained response equivalence or variance.

See Anderson, *op. cit.,* 126. Emphases are in the original.

19. Lehman, *op. cit.,* 368. Emphases are in the original.

20. The universalistic administration of law may turn into administration on behalf of particular interests; that is, political decision making removed from the arenas of political accountability. See, for instance, Theodore Lowi, "The Public Philosophy: Interest Group Liberalism," *American Political Science Review,* 61 (March 1967) 5-24. Also, see Theodore Lowi, *The End of Liberalism* (New York: Norton, 1969); and Murray Edelman, *The Symbolic Uses of Politics*

(Urbana: The University of Illinois Press, 1964). For a useful critique of various "models" of administrative conduct, see Glendon Schubert, *The Public Interest* (Glencoe, Ill.: The Free Press, 1960).

21. See, Torodd Strand, "Expertise, Innovation, and Influence," *Scandinavian Political Studies,* 4 (1969) 117-132. See, also, Thomas J. Anton, "Policy Making and Political Culture in Sweden," *Scandinavian Political Studies* 4 (1969) 88-102. More generally, the Scandinavian countries have been discussed in terms of a unified political culture and in particular a high degree of normative consensus among elites. With respect to Norway, see G. Lowell Field and John Higley, *Elites in Developed Societies: Theoretical Reflections on an Initial Stage in Norway* (Beverly Hills: Sage Publications, 1972); and Harry Eckstein, *Division and Cohesion in Democracy: A Study of Norway* (Princeton, N. J.: Princeton University Press, 1966).

22. The costs of dealing directly with broad value and perceptual influences in examining decision making can be debilitating operationally. On this score, see Richard C. Snyder, H. W. Bruck, and Burton Sapin, *Foreign Policy Decision Making: An Approach to the Study of International Politics* (Glencoe, Ill.: The Free Press, 1962) 14-185. If the case analyses cumulate, however, it may be possible to glean a set of "policy-culture" expectations. See here, Thomas J. Anton, "Incrementalism in Utopia: The Political Integration of Metropolitan Stockholm," *Urban Affairs Quarterly,* 5 (September 1969) 59-82. Of particular interest in this regard also is Charles O. Jones, "Doing Before Knowing: Concept Development in Political Research," *American Journal of Political Science,* 18 (February 1974) 215-228.

23. For a contrast of the comparative method and the case method, see Arend Lijphart, "Comparative Politics and the Comparative Method," *American Political Science Review,* 65 (September 1971) 682-693.

24. On this point, see Angus Campbell, "Voters and Elections: Past and Present," *Journal of Politics,* 26 (November 1964) especially 756.

25. As Richard Sisson observes, ". . . the more responsive an executive elite and the more adaptive a legislature, the more 'diluted' the output of a political system may be . . . " See Richard Sisson, "Comparative Legislative Institutionalization: A Theoretical Exploration," in Allan Kornberg (ed.), *Legislatures in Comparative Perspective* (New York: David McKay, 1973) 38.

26. Trust toward political authority is likely to diminish under the highly abrasive competition of demands and counter-demands. Yet, trust is a resource that is necessary to obtain compromise. See, for instance, Joel D. Aberbach and Jack L. Walker, "Political Trust and Racial Ideology," *American Political Science Review,* 64 (December 1970) especially 1215, *passim.*

27. Samuel P. Huntington, *Political Order in Changing Societies* (New Haven: Yale University Press, 1968) 110-111.

28. Jacob, *et al., op. cit.,* 4.

Augsburg College
George Sverdrup Library
Minneapolis, Minnesota 55454